In the Name of Allah the Gracious, the Merciful

Copyright © 2022 by Lantern Publications

All rights reserved. No part of this publication may be reproduced, distributed, or transmitted in any form or by any means, including photocopying, recording, or other electronic or mechanical methods, without the prior written permission of the publisher, except in the case of brief quotations embodied in critical reviews and certain other noncommercial uses permitted by copyright law. For permission requests, write to the publisher, addressed "Attention: - Permissions (Abraham  spreads monotheism)," at the email address below.

LanternKids

Lantern Publications
info@lanternpublications.com
www.lanternkids.com.au

A catalogue record for this book is available from the National Library of Australia

Ordering Information:

Quantity sales. Special discounts are available on quantity purchases by corporations, associations, and others. For details, contact the distributor at
the address above.

Written by: Abbass Noureddin | **Illustrated by:** Amir Khan |
Translated by: Amal Abdallah | **Edited by:** Dr Abidali Mohamedali

ISBN- 978-1-922583-26-0
Abbreviations used in this book:
(ﷺ) Alayhis Salaam – May peace be upon him.
(ﷺ) Salallahu Alayhi wa Aalihi wa Sallam- May peace and blessings be upon him and his immaculate family

First Edition

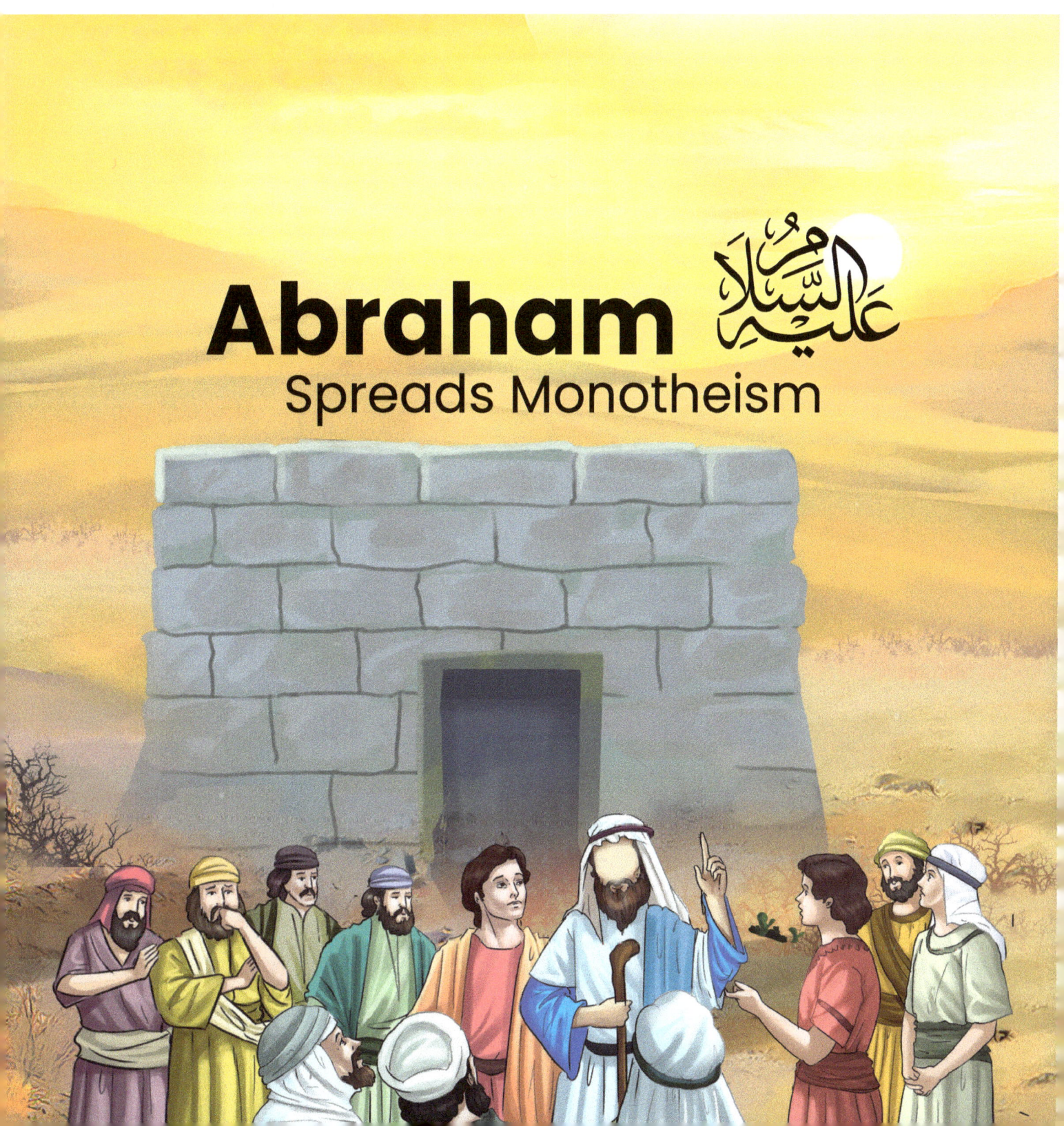

﴿إِنَّ إِبْرَاهِيمَ كَانَ أُمَّةً قَانِتًا لِلَّهِ حَنِيفًا وَلَمْ يَكُنْ مِنَ الْمُشْرِكِينَ﴾ النحل، الآية 120

"Indeed Abraham was a nation [all by himself], obedient to Allah, a Hanīf, and he was not a polytheist."
The Bee 16:120

Abraham Al-khalil (the friend) was a prophet of great intention and determination. He wished to change the world. He dreamt of saving people from all the wickedness and hardships from which they suffered. He knew that polytheism; that is worshipping other than God, is the origin of all evil and suffering.

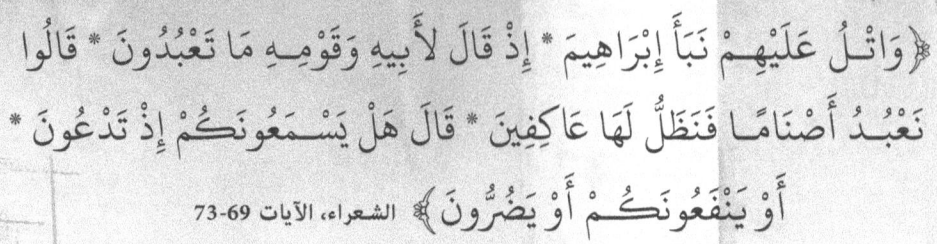

﴿وَاتْلُ عَلَيْهِمْ نَبَأَ إِبْرَاهِيمَ * إِذْ قَالَ لِأَبِيهِ وَقَوْمِهِ مَا تَعْبُدُونَ * قَالُوا نَعْبُدُ أَصْنَامًا فَنَظَلُّ لَهَا عَاكِفِينَ * قَالَ هَلْ يَسْمَعُونَكُمْ إِذْ تَدْعُونَ * أَوْ يَنْفَعُونَكُمْ أَوْ يَضُرُّونَ﴾ الشعراء، الآيات 69-73

"Relate to them the account of Abraham, when he said to his [adopted] father and his people, 'What is it that you are worshiping?!' They said, 'We worship idols, and are constant in our devotion to them.' He said, 'Do they hear you when you call them? Or do they bring you any benefit, or cause you any harm?'"
The Poets 26:69–73

Abraham ﷺ knew that if people worshipped idols they would not use their minds. If you glorify something that does not have the power to harm or benefit, it means that you become a slave to something that does not exist! This idol will not help you know what is good for you and what is bad.. Most problems and damage result from not using the mind.

﴿ قَالَ أَفَتَعْبُدُونَ مِن دُونِ اللَّهِ مَا لَا يَنفَعُكُمْ شَيْئًا وَلَا يَضُرُّكُمْ * أُفٍّ لَكُمْ وَلِمَا تَعْبُدُونَ مِن دُونِ اللَّهِ أَفَلَا تَعْقِلُونَ ﴾ الأنبياء، 66 ـ 67

﴿ فَجَعَلَهُمْ جُذَاذًا إِلَّا كَبِيرًا لَّهُمْ لَعَلَّهُمْ إِلَيْهِ يَرْجِعُونَ * قَالُوا مَن فَعَلَ هَذَا بِآلِهَتِنَا إِنَّهُ لَمِنَ الظَّالِمِينَ ﴾ الأنبياء، 58 ـ 59

"He said, 'Then, do you worship besides Allah that which cannot cause you any benefit or harm? Fie on you and what you worship besides Allah! Do you not exercise your reason?'"
The Prophets 21:66-67

"So he broke them [the idols] into pieces—all except the biggest of them—so that they might come back to it. They said, 'Whoever has done this to our gods?! He is indeed a wrongdoer!'"
The Prophets 21:58-59

Abraham ﷺ had a goal. He wanted to end the worship of idols. He started calling his people to worship no one but God. He wanted his people to go back to reason.
He went to where the idols were kept, and destroyed them all, except for the biggest one.
When the people came to the temple, and found that their idols were destroyed, they exclaimed," Who did this to our gods?"
Gods! Is it possible for a god to be broken or destroyed?!

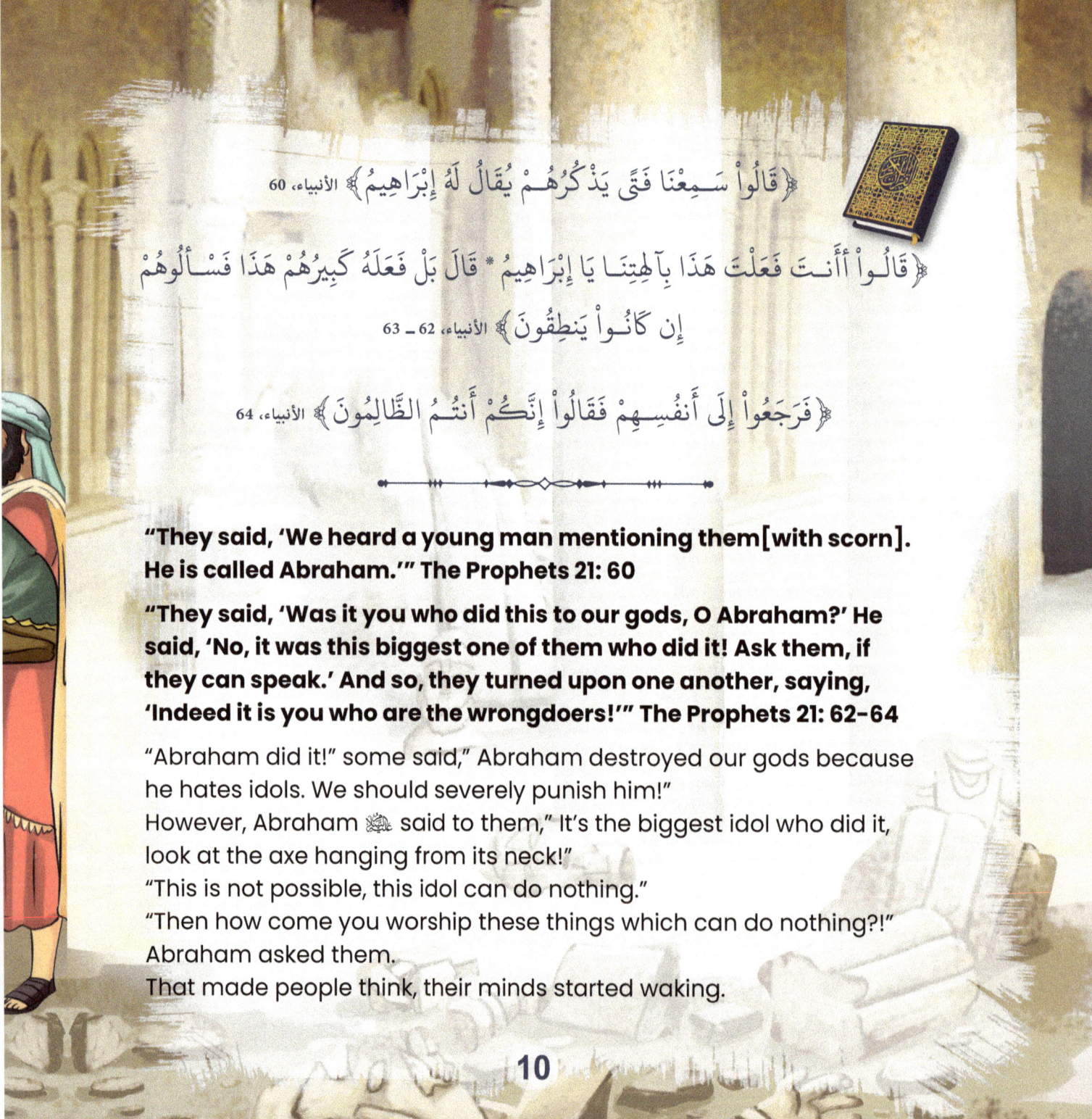

﴿ قَالُوا سَمِعْنَا فَتًى يَذْكُرُهُمْ يُقَالُ لَهُ إِبْرَاهِيمُ ﴾ الأنبياء، 60

﴿ قَالُوا أَأَنتَ فَعَلْتَ هَذَا بِآلِهَتِنَا يَا إِبْرَاهِيمُ * قَالَ بَلْ فَعَلَهُ كَبِيرُهُمْ هَذَا فَاسْأَلُوهُمْ إِن كَانُوا يَنطِقُونَ ﴾ الأنبياء، 62 - 63

﴿ فَرَجَعُوا إِلَى أَنفُسِهِمْ فَقَالُوا إِنَّكُمْ أَنتُمُ الظَّالِمُونَ ﴾ الأنبياء، 64

"They said, 'We heard a young man mentioning them [with scorn]. He is called Abraham.'" The Prophets 21: 60

"They said, 'Was it you who did this to our gods, O Abraham?' He said, 'No, it was this biggest one of them who did it! Ask them, if they can speak.' And so, they turned upon one another, saying, 'Indeed it is you who are the wrongdoers!'" The Prophets 21: 62-64

"Abraham did it!" some said," Abraham destroyed our gods because he hates idols. We should severely punish him!"
However, Abraham ﷺ said to them," It's the biggest idol who did it, look at the axe hanging from its neck!"
"This is not possible, this idol can do nothing."
"Then how come you worship these things which can do nothing?!" Abraham asked them.
That made people think, their minds started waking.

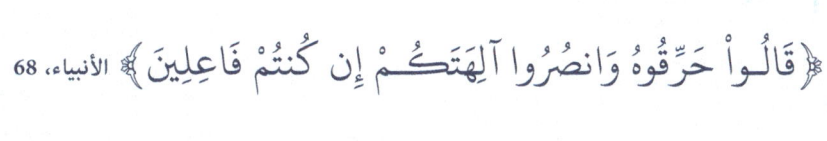

﴿ قَالُواْ حَرِّقُوهُ وَانصُرُوٓاْ ءَالِهَتَكُمْ إِن كُنتُمْ فَاعِلِينَ ﴾ الأنبياء، 68

"They said, 'Burn him, and help your gods, if you are to do anything!'" The Prophets 21:68

However, that incident was not enough for people to stop worshipping idols. They continued to obey Nemrod. Nemrod was a tyrant who ruled the people and controlled them through the idols. Nemrod told the people," We should punish Abraham if we don't want the gods to be furious. The gods will punish Abraham with fire."

And so they built a great fire to punish Abraham ﷺ. It was so great that its flames burned the birds hovering above it.
Then, they used a catapult to throw him into the fire.
After that, they waited for the fire to die.

﴿ قُلْنَا يَا نَارُ كُونِي بَرْدًا وَسَلَامًا عَلَى إِبْرَاهِيمَ ﴾ الأنبياء، 69

"We said, 'O fire! Be cool and safe for Abraham!'"
The Prophets 21: 69

Hours later, they came back. They could not believe what their eyes saw! It was Abraham ﷺ! They found him praying to God! He was untouched, the fire did not burn him! The flames were nothing but coolness and peace for Abraham ﷺ!
"Abraham's God is real, and our gods are fake." They said. Nemrod was afraid that he might lose control over the people, so he banished Abraham ﷺ. But it was too late, because the people had already started using their minds more and more.

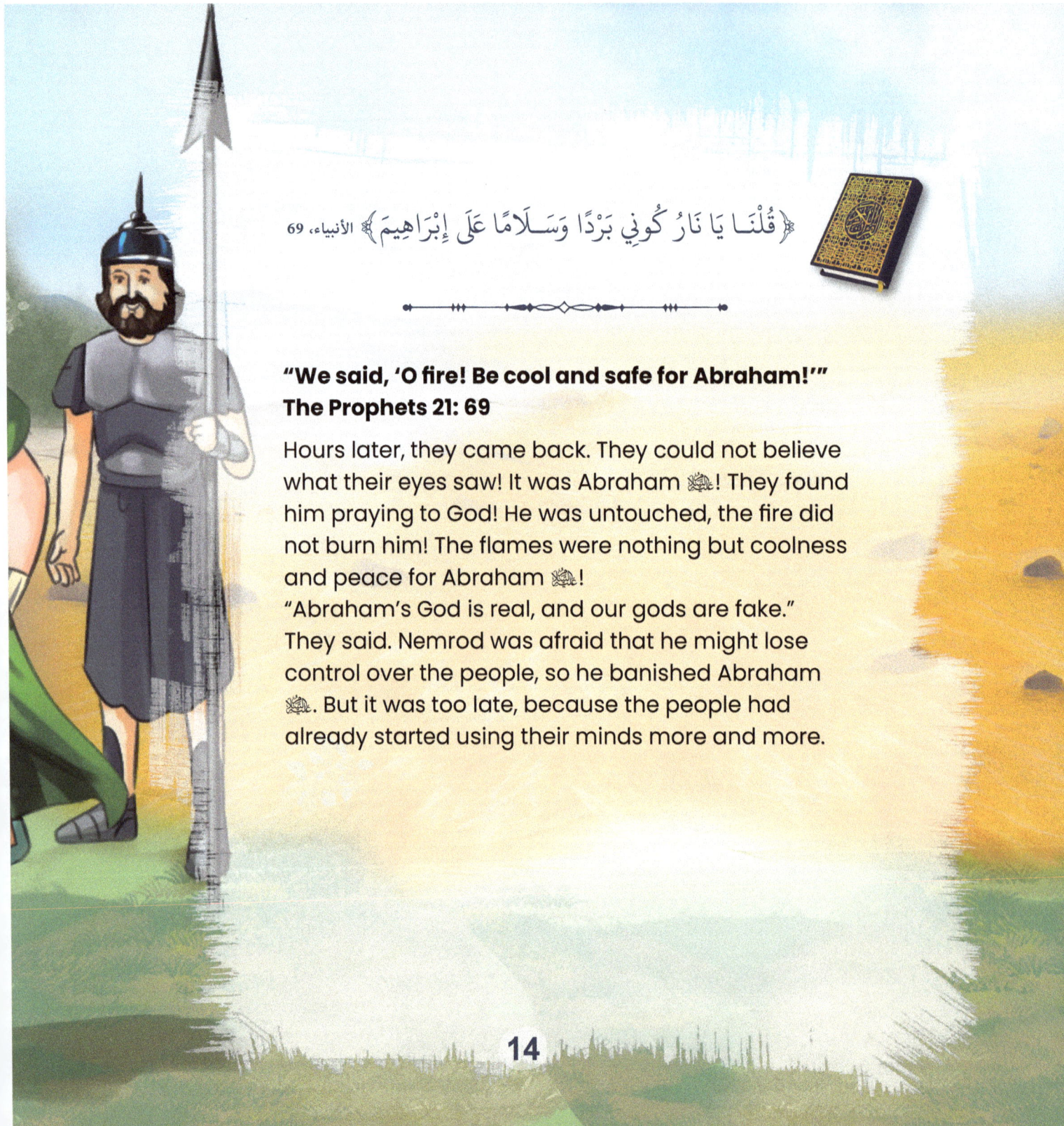

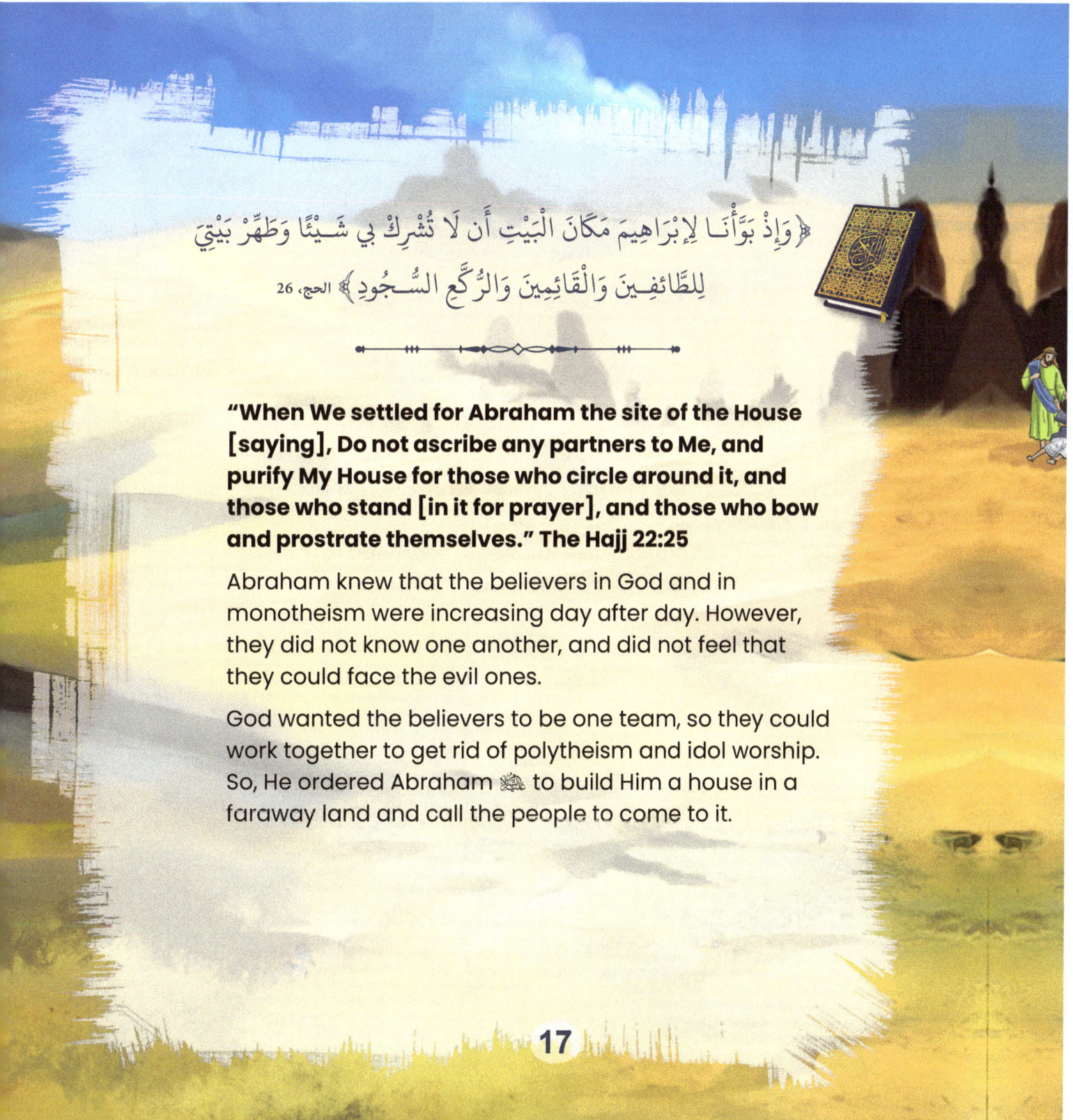

﴿وَإِذْ بَوَّأْنَا لِإِبْرَاهِيمَ مَكَانَ الْبَيْتِ أَن لَّا تُشْرِكْ بِي شَيْئًا وَطَهِّرْ بَيْتِيَ لِلطَّائِفِينَ وَالْقَائِمِينَ وَالرُّكَّعِ السُّجُودِ﴾ الحج، 26

"When We settled for Abraham the site of the House [saying], Do not ascribe any partners to Me, and purify My House for those who circle around it, and those who stand [in it for prayer], and those who bow and prostrate themselves." The Hajj 22:25

Abraham knew that the believers in God and in monotheism were increasing day after day. However, they did not know one another, and did not feel that they could face the evil ones.

God wanted the believers to be one team, so they could work together to get rid of polytheism and idol worship. So, He ordered Abraham ﷺ to build Him a house in a faraway land and call the people to come to it.

﴿ فَاتَّبِعُوا مِلَّةَ إِبْرَاهِيمَ حَنِيفًا وَمَا كَانَ مِنَ الْمُشْرِكِينَ ﴾ آل عمران، الآية 95

﴿ إِنَّ أَوَّلَ بَيْتٍ وُضِعَ لِلنَّاسِ لَلَّذِي بِبَكَّةَ مُبَارَكًا وَهُدًى لِلْعَالَمِينَ ﴾ آل عمران، الآية 96

﴿ فِيهِ آيَاتٌ بَيِّنَاتٌ مَقَامُ إِبْرَاهِيمَ وَمَنْ دَخَلَهُ كَانَ آمِنًا ﴾ آل عمران، الآية 97

"So follow the creed of Abraham, a Hanīf, and he was not one of the polytheists." Family of Imran 3:95
"Indeed the first house to be set up for mankind is the one at Bakkah, blessed and a guidance for all nations." Family of Imran 3:96
"In it are manifest signs [and] Abraham's Station, and whoever enters it shall be secure." Family of Imran 3:97

Abraham builds Al Kaaba.

Abraham dedicated all his life to God, and asked Allah, The Almighty, to tell him how to guide the people. God told Abraham ﷺ to examine his life in order to know the answer to his question. God said to Abraham ﷺ that people would be guided by his life, the life which Abraham totally dedicated to God. God also said that he would make Abraham's ﷺ house God's house as well.

﴿رَبَّنَا إِنِّي أَسْكَنْتُ مِنْ ذُرِّيَّتِي بِوَادٍ غَيْرِ ذِي زَرْعٍ عِنْدَ بَيْتِكَ الْمُحَرَّمِ رَبَّنَا لِيُقِيمُوا الصَّلَاةَ فَاجْعَلْ أَفْئِدَةً مِنَ النَّاسِ تَهْوِي إِلَيْهِمْ وَارْزُقْهُمْ مِنَ الثَّمَرَاتِ لَعَلَّهُمْ يَشْكُرُونَ﴾ إبراهيم، 37

"Our Lord! I have settled part of my descendants in a barren valley, by Your sacred House, our Lord, that they may maintain the prayer. So, make the hearts of a part of the people fond of them, and provide them with fruitful sustenance, so that they may give thanks."
Abraham 14:37

Abraham ﷺ together with his wife Hajar and son Ismail migrated to a barren land that had neither water nor plants. So, God made going to the pilgrimage of Hajj like Abraham's migration.
Abraham wanted to unite the believers, so God made The pilgrimage (Hajj) a means to unite believers. Abraham wanted to terminate polytheism and Idol worship, so God made The pilgrimage (Hajj) a means to abolish the worship of idols.

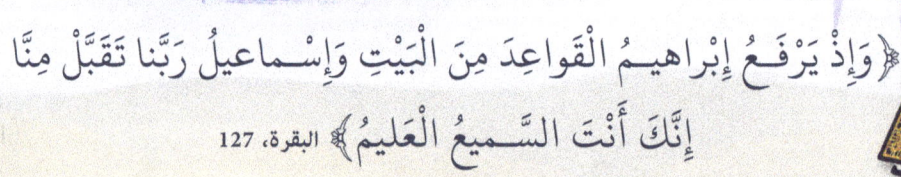

﴿وَإِذْ يَرْفَعُ إِبْرَاهِيمُ الْقَوَاعِدَ مِنَ الْبَيْتِ وَإِسْمَاعِيلُ رَبَّنَا تَقَبَّلْ مِنَّا إِنَّكَ أَنْتَ السَّمِيعُ الْعَلِيمُ﴾ البقرة، 127

"As Abraham raised the foundations of the House with Ishmael, [they prayed]: 'Our Lord, accept it from us! Indeed You are the All-hearing, the All-knowing."
The Cow 2: 127

Abraham built a house in Makah. He said, "I will make this the house of God."

Hajar started looking for water to quench Ismail's thirst. She started going back and forth between Safa and Marwa, until she came back to her baby Ismail, where she found water springing from under his feet. Hence, Makkah became a land with a water spring named Zamzam.

People started coming to Makkah. They found Ismail ﷺ worshiping God in His house, so they started learning about monotheism.

﴿وَأَذِّن فِي النَّاسِ بِالْحَجِّ يَأْتُوكَ رِجَالًا وَعَلَىٰ كُلِّ ضَامِرٍ يَأْتِينَ مِن كُلِّ فَجٍّ عَمِيقٍ﴾ الحج، 27

"And proclaim the Hajj to all the people: they will come to you on foot and on lean camels, coming from distant places." The Pilgrimage 22:27

Abraham sent out a great call to all the believers around the world, to come as pilgrims to Makkah, and learn the worship of the one and only God.

From that point onward, a great center for Monotheism was founded, to which believers travelled from all around the world, until Prophet Muhammad ﷺ came. Prophet Muhammad ﷺ said," I am the call of Abraham, and I will make the Kaaba the center for changing the world."

So, how did this change start, and where did it reach? We will learn this in coming stories.